This book is dedicated to m
who returned to heaven on December 17, 2000.

"You have filled my life with love and many beautiful memories."

Sadie was an Olde English Sheepdog rescued as a puppy
from the SPCA in my hometown of Norfolk, Virginia

Sadie
The Guardian Angel:
Do Dogs Go To Heaven?

Story by Lawrence E. Lambert

Illustrations by
Charity Russell

How An Angel Gets A Name

Angels come to earth
And look like you and me
You cannot tell their divine nature
There is nothing you can see
You find them by watching the things they do
The gifts they offer both me and you
Their loving hearts
Their giving ways
The way they bring light to the darkest days

Angels come and Angels go
Teaching us lessons of life
And when the sun has almost set
The Angel's job is not over yet
And as they depart
In sweet refrain
We discover that Angel had a name

In a time not so long ago an angel fell in love with a little boy.
This young angel was assigned the task of watching over a child
on the day of his birth. From the first moment she saw him,
she fell hopelessly in love with the little baby boy. Each night
before he would go to sleep the little angel would sing to him a
special song of love and protection.

Don't be afraid
Don't be afraid of the dark
I will always be with you
I won't let the darkness through
I will always be your shining light
And when the darkness comes
And sand gets in your eyes
I will always be with you until sunrise
Don't be afraid of the dark.

Through the months, the little angel was there to watch over the little boy.

She saw him stand for the first time and take his first steps.

The little angel stood guard and watched the event with both pride and joy.

She promised to never be far from her little boy,

especially now that he was learning to walk and falling all the time.

Weeks later the little angel was there to hear his first words...

just the little angel and his mother.

The young angel was there the day when he almost fell down

the stairs. She tried to stop him, but he walked right through

her. His mother saw him out of the corner of her eye and was

able to catch him before he could reach the stairs.

"Phew!", sighed the angel.

The little angel watched this event with both joy and sadness.

Joy that he was swept away from danger, and sadness that

she was not able to stop him from falling down the stairs.

Although she could watch him every day, sadly, she

could never touch her little boy as his guardian angel.

All she could do was sing, and sing she did, every night until he would

close his eyes and fall asleep.

Each night, the little angel wished she could rock him to sleep, just like

his mother.

"If only I could hold him in my arms. I would have been

able to keep him from falling down the stairs."

The little angel sighed, "How am I going to keep him safe?"

Days passed quickly and in time the baby she loved so deeply

grew into a rambunctious little boy.

Since he was an active little boy he was always busy playing and at night when it was time to rest, he would protest and cry. His little eyes would look so heavy that he could barely keep them open. Only the angel's singing would ease his frustration and help him to sleep. The little angel felt such pride that her voice could magically stop his crying and help him sleep.

The little boy was afraid of many things during this time. He was scared of strangers and spiders, but mostly he was afraid of the dark. But the little angel loved him anyway and she made things seem brighter at night for her little boy. Her love grew more and more each day because he needed her.

Each night at bedtime the little angel would sing to him. Although he could not hear her, he would hum along and soon be asleep.

The little boy liked to do scary things at this age. He liked to jump

and tumble on his bed and climb trees. One day, the little boy was

outside swinging so high on his new swing that the little angel

feared that he would fall and hurt himself.

"How am I going to keep such an active child safe?",

sighed the little angel.

She tried to warn him to be careful, but he could not hear her.

As the little angel feared, she watched him lose his grip and fall.

She frantically tried to catch him, but she could not keep her

little boy from falling.

The little boy and the angel were lucky that day. He only scraped

his elbow and knee.

"How am I going to protect him?", cried the little angel.

"If I could only touch him, then I would be able to keep him safe."

Every day she feared more and more that she needed to be able to

touch her little boy to keep him safe.

So the little angel went to talk with the oldest and wisest angel in heaven.

Her name was Precious.

"It is very rare for an guardian angel to have a name," thought the little angel.

"Precious surely will be able to help me."

Precious was the most beautiful angel the little angel had ever seen.

Precious had been the guardian for many children in her day. The little angel asked the wise old angel how she could hold her little boy in her arms. She was convinced that she could be a better guardian angel if she could only touch her little boy and pick him up. Precious smiled and reached out to take the hand of the little angel.

"There is only one way for a guardian angel to touch the child they are assigned to protect," said the wise old angel.

A very serious look appeared on the old angel's face, and she said, "To be a part of your child's world, you must give up your wings and halo and your place in heaven. For your sacrifice you will be able to touch your little boy."

"Heed this warning and make your decision carefully,"

said the wise old angel.

"There will be joy and happiness, as well as pain and disappointment;

and only one way back to heaven."

"Remember, although you can touch your little boy, you will not be able to

pick him up and hold him in your arms like his mother."

"Will I be able to protect my little boy?" asked the little angel.

"Yes," Precious said with a smile. "You will be able to protect him, teach him

how to care about others, and give him lots of love and affection.

But, remember your time on his earth will be short!"

"Will I be able to sing to him?" asked the little angel.

"Yes," Precious said, "but he won't be able to understand you. Think long

and hard about what I've said and make your decision carefully."

"I will do it!" yelled the little angel.

A few days later on the boy's seventh birthday, his Mother surprised

him with a puppy. It was a tiny puppy with soft white and black fur

and sparkling brown eyes. His mother taught him how to hold the

puppy and the little angel felt relieved.

He decided that he would call her "Sadie".

At first it was hard being a puppy.

The little angel was used to hovering above her little boy without any

effort. Now she had to get her wobbly paws to stay under her on the

wooden floors. Many times she would slip while trying to learn how

to walk.

"I can understand why my little boy had trouble with walking,"

thought the little angel. The strangest thing was the rumbling sensation

in her stomach. The perk was the delicious food they gave her to cure

the feeling. But with all good things, the angel learned that what went in

her mouth came out the other end. And the little angel felt bad when

she made a mess on the carpet.

She also felt terrible about chewing on her boy's shoes and socks. But she could not control herself. They smelled just like him and she loved playing with his shoes and most of all with the little boy.

"Giving up my wings was a small price for my floppy ears and soft coat," thought the little angel. She knew her little boy liked rubbing her head and calling her new name. She especially liked the belly rubs and the scratching behind her ears. Precious had never mentioned the pure joy of being able to touch and cuddle with your little boy.

At night they kept her in the kitchen so she would sing to him until he would sneak her up to his room.

She was the happiest angel indeed.

"Nothing bad," she barked, "will ever happen to my little boy now that I am here to protect him."

As a puppy, she loved singing to him every night even though he could

not understand the song anymore. He would rub her head and she

would lick his face. In time, Sadie stopped singing the song.

Neither the little boy nor his mother seemed to like her nightly singing.

The inseparable pair loved to play all day, running along the fields near

his house. The little boy would pull Sadie around the yard in his wagon.

The angel felt so happy that she could be there to watch her little boy

and keep him safe. In just a few months Sadie grew, and grew, and grew

into a strong protector. Never had Sadie felt such joy and happiness.

Finally, she was able to touch her little boy every day. It was a dream

come true for the little guardian angel.

In time, Sadie grew too large to be pulled around in his wagon.

Soon it was Sadie's turn to pull him around.

"Hold on tight!" Sadie would bark as she pulled him up and

down the street in front of their house. Sadie took the job of

being his protector very seriously. She was there to warn him

of danger when their doorbell rang or when someone turned

on the "loud sucking bag".

She especially hated the "soapy water maker" in the laundry room.

She attended to her job of protection with great care. Each day

Sadie was dedicated to fill his heart with love and affection.

Sadie was there to hear him cry when he felt sad or if he scraped his knee.

She was even there to lick his face when he needed some affection.

"What a wonderful life!", barked the little angel.

Many, many nights she would race him up the stairs and jump on his bed.

Silently, she would curl up next to him while he slept.

In time, he was eight, then nine and then ten.

Sadie was grateful that she could be there to care for her little boy.

He told her secrets that he never told anyone else.

Sadie would keep all his secrets and never tell a soul.

The years went by quickly and soon Sadie found that it was getting

harder to keep up with her little boy.

"Oh boy he's fast!", Sadie barked as she ran behind him.

"Wait up!" she panted as they ran back to the house.

"Keeping up with a twelve year old is not an easy task,"

woofed the little angel.

On the boy's thirteenth birthday, Sadie felt especially sore. He had

gotten a skateboard for his birthday and Sadie pulled him around

on his new toy all day. That night she remembered the warnings of

Precious, but quickly put it out of her mind.

"I've just got to keep up with the little boy," she thought."

At night she especially liked sleeping next to him. She was there to

listen for all sounds of danger. She could hear a cat or another dog

from blocks away. Sadie would bark her warning and he would call

her name and soon they would both be asleep.

In a few short years, Sadie's little boy was sixteen.

Her days of pulling him around in his wagon or on his skateboard were over. Her old bones and sore muscles had lost their strength. He was now pulling her around in his wagon again.

At bedtime he would help Sadie up the stairs and onto his bed. During these days she worried about who would watch him if something happened to her.

The words of the wise old angel came back to haunt her every day. Sadie felt her vision fading and feared that soon she would not be able to watch her boy. Each day she questioned her decision to be with him, but it was too late now. Every day she struggled to stay close, but she just couldn't keep up.

"Who will watch my little boy?" she whined as she struggled to follow him around the house.

"Oh! I have made a terrible mistake!", cried the little angel as she feared her furry body would soon fail her.

Eight days before Christmas the boy carried her up the stairs and carefully put her on his bed. Sadie felt so tired that she could barely hold up her head. When she heard the boy singing, she thought she was dreaming. She hadn't thought about the song in many years, but remembered it right away. She gathered the strength to lift her head to sing along.

Don't be afraid
Don't be afraid of the dark
I will always be with you
I won't let the darkness through
I will always be your shining light
And when the darkness comes
And sand gets in your eyes
I will always be with you until sunrise
Don't be afraid of the dark.

Soon the boy was asleep. When Sadie was about to join him she heard
a strange sound in the kitchen. To her surprise Sadie found the strength
to get out of his bed and make her way down the stairs. With each
step the sound grew louder and louder until she found herself
surrounded by the singing of Angels.

One angel came closer and Sadie remembered the face of Precious.

"Congratulations! Sadie, you have earned your place back in heaven,"

Precious said.

"You have made the ultimate sacrifice any angel can make.

You were willing to give up your place in heaven to protect

your little boy in a time when he most needed you."

"You have given him love and taught him how to love and care about others. For this generous deed you have earned your wings and halo and a place of honor back in heaven. From this moment on you will be known as Sadie, The Guardian Angel."

To Sadie's surprise she shed her fur and became an angel again, but now she was all grown up and beautiful like Precious.

"But what will happen to my little boy?" asked Sadie.

"Your job is not over," said Precious. "He will be very sad now, and you must go and let him know that you are okay."

"How will I let him know that I am okay?" asked Sadie.

"You will know what to do," said Precious with a smile.

Instantly, Sadie found herself sitting at the foot of the bed of her

little boy. She could hear him crying for her.

"Don't be sad," Sadie said as she filled his heart with love.

Then she cleared her voice and began to sing.

Don't be afraid
Don't be afraid of the dark
I will always be with you
I won't let the darkness through
I will always be your shining light.
And when the darkness comes
And sand gets in your eyes
I will always be with you until sunrise
Don't be afraid of the dark
Your Sadie will watch over you
and protect you from danger
while you sleep.

And soon her little boy was asleep.

The End

So you ask if dogs go to heaven. Of course they do...

All angels belong in heaven.

A dog is the perfect reflection of God's love.

Just reverse the letters and you will see.

DOG becomes GOD.

Amen

Attach a picture of your pet angel.

Made in the USA
Columbia, SC
10 October 2017